90 Days
to Your
Better Self

An Interactive Guide to
Self-realization and Healing

Sylviette D. McGill, B.S., M.Ed., TESL

PAGE PUBLISHING, INC.
Conneaut Lake, PA

First originally published by Page Publishing 2020

Cover Photo Credit: Sylviette D. McGill of Del's Photography
One-of-a-Kind Canvas Series www.delscanvas-series.com

ISBN 978-1-6624-2129-7 (pbk)
ISBN 978-1-6624-2130-3 (digital)

Printed in the United States of America

This book is dedicated to the memory of my grandparents.

Bishop Robert Lee Graham (1913–1988) and
Elder Mary Smith Graham (1918–1997)

Mr. Tom Arthur Nicholson (1909–2003) and
Mrs. Nettie Burnett Nicholson (1913–2014)

My sister:

Glenda Louise Nicholson (1954–1997)

Preface

Introducing you to your better self in ninety days is already exciting for me! I've taken thirty years of lessons learned, discoveries made, realities faced, and condensed them into this book so it doesn't take you as long as it took me. Granted the format is just a bit unorthodox because I'm not simply telling you what I learned, but I presented everything in a way that causes you to look inside yourself, not inside me. The daily guides collectively stimulate thought and help you understand things about yourself. Carve out time to spend with yourself if you don't already. Create a group to share with others if you only spend time with yourself. Schedule date nights with yourself. Take walks in the park in thought, and then sit and write responses in your book. Go to a coffee shop alone to work on yourself. Schedule a meeting with yourself if you're always scheduling with someone else. Take an hour after work to sit in the car before driving home, and strengthen your connection with yourself.

That's why this interactive book is about getting in closer contact with yourself, which automatically creates your better self. This book is not a passive read at all! It's not about escaping to a foreign land, peeping into the lives of imaginary characters—as a matter of fact, it's the exact opposite. I strongly suggest that you choose ninety days of a particular season to transition your better self. Of course, if you want to start right away and you've received your book in the middle of spring then, by all means, don't hesitate. For the next three months, you will be under the lamp of self-discovery. You will learn new things about yourself and advance the things you already know about yourself to become the better you that you've been waiting on. Think of it as a gift to yourself and, as a gift to those that you love and respect.

Additionally, don't hesitate to invite anyone along this road to freedom with you, and if you find that you want to expand that idea even further, I encourage you to form groups—or even a book club—and increase the interaction. But remember, when sharing, you're only focusing on sharing about you. This is not designed for you to critique others (not unless they ask) because we don't want to get off the theme of "you," which is easier for some than others. The main thing about sharing and hearing others in their self-discoveries is that you may get ideas about yourself that you weren't aware of, or it may stimulate thought processes that had never occurred to you. The idea is that, when you improve upon yourself, you automatically improve your life. Everything jumps to the next level. When you seek, discover, grasp, and then glean in on your purpose in life, you maximize the journey while simultaneously inspiring those around you to do the same. Imagine that there's nothing more satisfying than looking back on your life and seeing how far you've traveled. In this journey called "life," we either take charge and insist upon becoming more conscious each day, or we remain passive and let life take us where it wants to go—with no control of the wheel.

Even though this is a ninety-day interactive guide, it doesn't require that you journal/record in chronological order, which is why I put a line for dates that you actually perform a daily. Also, if your schedule is too hectic to write on a daily basis, then I would suggest that you set aside time for yourself on the weekend and perform seven dailies consecutively. I wouldn't suggest going past seven days because some of the work is very challenging when you're required to see things about yourself that you don't want to see and then the work that it takes to change the behavior that you choose to change. When you are forced to write it down or record it verbally, it can be exhausting. Anytime you feel fatigue, just get excited because it's indicative of the process at work. You can be confident that you are well on your way to your better self. Now, the irony is this, once you've arrived at your destination of your better self, you could do this self-help guide again, and your responses will be more developed, which is also a reflection of the work you've done to give yourself the best self that you possibly can.

Good luck.

Note: Each day has space for you to write your responses, but if there are days that you have a lot to write, I've added a few blank pages at the back of the book; and then if you are really in an overflow of your personal work, please don't hesitate to get a companion notebook to complete your assignments. For those of you who prefer to speak rather than write, please feel free to record your verbal responses on any device that you have available. Second, some days don't have specific instructions like others do; in these cases, I purposefully designed that you use that designated word, phrase, or sentence, and either turn it into a question for yourself or simply write from within as it relates to that topic. I have learned that because our work can be so different that the same word can mean something different to the next person, and this is where it is vital that you write from your internal place on topics that are not so specific so that it gives you the freedom to dig up unconscious substances that lie within.

Introduction

In my twenties, I knew I wanted to write a best seller; but in my fifties, I understand why any major success would have separated me further from myself. This guide isn't about selling a certain number of books, it's about doing my personal work in spiritual development, which in return develops all the other areas of life which forms alignment with the Creator and gets us all on purpose for our lives. This, my friend, is what I'm convinced is missing from most of our planning in life; sometimes, we're trying to attract things we are not ready for ourselves. I have discovered that without the correct state of mind and the proper spiritual alignment, God will put certain success on hold because He knows ultimately it can completely destroy us! And we know that all things work together for good to them that love God, to them who are the called according to his purpose (Romans 8:28 KJV). So by now, you have suspected that I believe in God, or as some may refer to, a Higher Power. And even though this book is not about your religious preference (or no), it's about what you do believe, and measuring how your beliefs play a role in your existence.

I have an unyielding confidence that this collection of thought-provoking passages will stimulate your will and open mind to gravitate to your better self! Congratulations in advance!

GUIDED EXERCISES TO YOUR BETTER SELF

Day 1

Is your past in the past, or have you insisted upon dragging it into this moment? If you do not want to let go of the past, why? If you have, what lessons have you brought to this moment?

Date: _____

_____

_____

_____

_____

_____

_____

_____

_____

_____

_____

_____

_____

_____

_____

_____

_____

_____

_____

_____

_____

_____

_____

_____

Sylviette D. McGill, B.S., M.Ed., TESL

Day 2

Healing can oftentimes be painful! That's why so many of
us try to avoid dealing with challenges instead of facing
the enemy of ourselves. And many times, this flee results
in denial. Talk about what you're in denial with.

Date: _____

_____

_____
_____
_____
_____
_____
_____
_____
_____
_____
_____
_____
_____
_____
_____
_____
_____
_____
_____
_____
_____

Sylviette D. McGill, B.S., M.Ed., TESL

Day 3

Integrity!
What lies do you constantly tell yourself, and what
truths do you constantly tell yourself?

Date: _____

_____

_____
_____
_____
_____
_____
_____
_____
_____
_____
_____
_____
_____
_____
_____
_____
_____
_____
_____
_____
_____
_____
_____
_____

Sylviette D. McGill, B.S., M.Ed., TESL

Day 4

If life is a journey of emotional, psychological, physical, and/or
spiritual healing, what would you say is your greatest challenge?
Who should you hold responsible for movement
in your life besides yourself?

Date: _____

_____

_____
_____
_____
_____
_____
_____
_____
_____
_____
_____
_____
_____
_____
_____
_____
_____
_____
_____
_____
_____
_____

Sylviette D. McGill, B.S., M.Ed., TESL

Day 5

Trust. Can you? Do you? When the issue of trust surfaces, one can usually find an issue of pain is associated with it.

Date: _____

_____

_____
_____
_____
_____
_____
_____
_____
_____
_____
_____
_____
_____
_____
_____
_____
_____
_____
_____
_____
_____
_____
_____

Sylviette D. McGill, B.S., M.Ed., TESL

Day 6

Today is a new day! It is also an opportunity to start
something you know you need to do. What is it?
What's the first step that you will be taking today?

Date: _____

_____

_____
_____
_____
_____
_____
_____
_____
_____
_____
_____
_____
_____
_____
_____
_____
_____
_____
_____
_____
_____

Sylviette D. McGill, B.S., M.Ed., TESL

Day 7

As you climb to your next level in life, allow
your heart to say "thank you" to the people who
have helped you arrive at this juncture.

Date: _____

_____

_____
_____
_____
_____
_____
_____
_____
_____
_____
_____
_____
_____
_____
_____
_____
_____
_____
_____
_____
_____
_____

Day 8

What does "love" mean to you?

Date: _____

_____

_____

_____

_____

_____

_____

_____

_____

_____

_____

_____

_____

_____

_____

_____

_____

_____

_____

_____

_____

_____

_____

_____

_____

_____

_____

_____

_____

Sylviette D. McGill, B.S., M.Ed., TESL

Day 9

Do you love yourself?

Date: _____

_____

_____

_____

_____

_____

_____

_____

_____

_____

_____

_____

_____

_____

_____

_____

_____

_____

_____

_____

_____

_____

_____

_____

_____

_____

_____

_____
_____
_____
_____
_____
_____
_____
_____
_____
_____
_____
_____
_____
_____
_____
_____
_____
_____
_____
_____
_____
_____
_____
_____
_____
_____
_____
_____
_____
_____
_____
_____
_____
_____

Day 10

Are you living your life or someone else's?

Date: _____

_____

_____

_____

_____

_____

_____

_____

_____

_____

_____

_____

_____

_____

_____

_____

_____

_____

_____

_____

_____

_____

_____

_____

_____

_____

Sylviette D. McGill, B.S., M.Ed., TESL

Day 11

Many assert that we should be grateful for the good and what we so oftentimes consider bad. What "bad" are you grateful for today?

Date: _____

_____

_____
_____
_____
_____
_____
_____
_____
_____
_____
_____
_____
_____
_____
_____
_____
_____
_____
_____
_____
_____
_____

Sylviette D. McGill, B.S., M.Ed., TESL

Day 12

How do you teach yourself how to have a bad day
with so much of the society placing an emphasis
on everything looking good all the time?

Date: _____

Sylviette D. McGill, B.S., M.Ed., TESL

Day 13

Oftentimes, many of us spend so much of our time trying to make life comfortable. Talk about ways that comfort can impede your growth, stifle your goals, and distract your vision.

Date: _____

_____

_____
_____
_____
_____
_____
_____
_____
_____
_____
_____
_____
_____
_____
_____
_____
_____
_____
_____
_____
_____
_____

Sylviette D. McGill, B.S., M.Ed., TESL

Day 14

You are alive today! What would you do differently
today if you knew you wouldn't be alive tomorrow?

Date: _____

_____

_____

_____

_____

_____

_____

_____

_____

_____

_____

_____

_____

_____

_____

_____

_____

_____

_____

_____

_____

_____

_____

_____

Sylviette D. McGill, B.S., M.Ed., TESL

Day 15

Disappointment is not an enemy. I am thoroughly convinced that it is a friend because it's a signal that something about you is out of alignment. Identify a memorable disappointment and talk about what it revealed to you about you.

Date: _____

_____

_____
_____
_____
_____
_____
_____
_____
_____
_____
_____
_____
_____
_____
_____
_____
_____
_____
_____
_____
_____
_____

Sylviette D. McGill, B.S., M.Ed., TESL

Day 16

Those who are not looking for happiness are the most likely to find it, because those who are searching forget that the surest way to be happy is to seek happiness for others.

—Martin Luther King Jr.

Date: _____

_____

_____
_____
_____
_____
_____
_____
_____
_____
_____
_____
_____
_____
_____
_____
_____
_____
_____
_____

Sylviette D. McGill, B.S., M.Ed., TESL

Day 17

"The fault, dear Brutus, lies not within the stars, but in ourselves, that we are underlings."

—Julius Caesar Act 1, Scene 2; *Shakespeare*

Date: _____

_____

_____
_____
_____
_____
_____
_____
_____
_____
_____
_____
_____
_____
_____
_____
_____
_____
_____
_____
_____
_____

Sylviette D. McGill, B.S., M.Ed., TESL

Day 18

Do we see in ourselves what we see in others? Oftentimes, we possess an unconscious tendency to highlight a quality that we have in someone else, whether negative or positive! Today, write about a negative feature that nags you about someone else, and then identify it in your life and list three ways you're going to change it.

Date: _____

_____

_____
_____
_____
_____
_____
_____
_____
_____
_____
_____
_____
_____
_____
_____
_____
_____
_____
_____
_____
_____
_____

Sylviette D. McGill, B.S., M.Ed., TESL

Day 19

Never deny the truth of who you are! We're talking the good, the bad, and the ugly! It's you! But guess what, you have purpose here in this earth, and it's about getting to your best self. Talk about whether or not you have discovered your purpose in life.

Date: _____

_____

_____
_____
_____
_____
_____
_____
_____
_____
_____
_____
_____
_____
_____
_____
_____
_____
_____
_____
_____
_____
_____
_____

Sylviette D. McGill, B.S., M.Ed., TESL

Day 20

Today is tough because your assignment is to find a set of
people in your life who are generally truthful, whether it's your
workplace, church, fitness group, book club, etc., and ask ten
people to comment on your persona. Ask them to be honest
(because you are doing a personality development work) and
tell, text, e-mail you as to their perceptions of you. In your
space, write about ways in which you agree or disagree with
the observations! (You may want a glass of wine tonight!)

Date: _____

_____

_____
_____
_____
_____
_____
_____
_____
_____
_____
_____
_____
_____
_____

Sylviette D. McGill, B.S., M.Ed., TESL

Day 21

Write about what you see when you look at yourself in the mirror.

Date: _____

_____

_____

_____

_____

_____

_____

_____

_____

_____

_____

_____

_____

_____

_____

_____

_____

_____

_____

_____

_____

_____

_____

_____

_____

_____

_____

Sylviette D. McGill, B.S., M.Ed., TESL

Day 22

Would you consider yourself positive or negative based? Don't measure this based on others, only in what you evaluate about yourself!
Note: Reference negative and positive charges.

Date: _____

_____
_____
_____
_____
_____
_____
_____
_____
_____
_____
_____
_____
_____
_____
_____
_____
_____
_____
_____
_____
_____
_____
_____

Sylviette D. McGill, B.S., M.Ed., TESL

Day 23

In the area of spirituality, what is your core belief?
If you don't have one, write about that.

Date: _____

_____

_____

_____

_____

_____

_____

_____

_____

_____

_____

_____

_____

_____

_____

_____

_____

_____

_____

_____

_____

_____

_____

_____

_____

_____

Sylviette D. McGill, B.S., M.Ed., TESL

Day 24

What do you believe about divine justice in the universe?

Date: _____

_____

_____
_____
_____
_____
_____
_____
_____
_____
_____
_____
_____
_____
_____
_____
_____
_____
_____
_____
_____
_____
_____
_____
_____
_____
_____

Sylviette D. McGill, B.S., M.Ed., TESL

Day 25

How much control do you believe you have in your life?

Date: _____

_____

_____

_____

_____

_____

_____

_____

_____

_____

_____

_____

_____

_____

_____

_____

_____

_____

_____

_____

_____

_____

_____

_____

Sylviette D. McGill, B.S., M.Ed., TESL

Day 26

When you are faced with challenges, do you greet them
realizing that they are a part of life, or do you avoid
them as if they are an inconvenience of life?

Date: _____

_____

_____
_____
_____
_____
_____
_____
_____
_____
_____
_____
_____
_____
_____
_____
_____
_____
_____
_____
_____
_____
_____

Sylviette D. McGill, B.S., M.Ed., TESL

Day 27

Write about the best way(s) that you learn
(audio, kinesthetic, visual).

Date: _____

_____

_____
_____
_____
_____
_____
_____
_____
_____
_____
_____
_____
_____
_____
_____
_____
_____
_____
_____
_____
_____
_____
_____

Sylviette D. McGill, B.S., M.Ed., TESL

Day 28

"Be the change that you wish to see in the world."

—Mahatma Gandhi

What change are you?

Date: _____

_____

_____
_____
_____
_____
_____
_____
_____
_____
_____
_____
_____
_____
_____
_____
_____
_____
_____
_____
_____
_____

Sylviette D. McGill, B.S., M.Ed., TESL

Day 29

If beauty is truly in the eye of the beholder, what is it that you
see when you look at yourself? List the things that you see.
And then a list of the contrary.

Date: _____

_____

_____
_____
_____
_____
_____
_____
_____
_____
_____
_____
_____
_____
_____
_____
_____
_____
_____
_____
_____
_____

Sylviette D. McGill, B.S., M.Ed., TESL

Day 30

Considering the idea that it takes thirty days of consistent repetition to change things about ourselves, let's put it to the test. Take one of the not-so-beautiful things from your previous list and practice the exact opposite for the next thirty days, and then return to this page and talk about your better self!

Date: _____

_____

_____
_____
_____
_____
_____
_____
_____
_____
_____
_____
_____
_____
_____
_____
_____
_____
_____
_____
_____
_____
_____
_____

Sylviette D. McGill, B.S., M.Ed., TESL

Day 31

Whether it's the flowers or the rain, the trees or the
snow, the sun or the stars, what is it about nature
that stimulates you the most, and why?

Date: _____

_____

_____
_____
_____
_____
_____
_____
_____
_____
_____
_____
_____
_____
_____
_____
_____
_____
_____
_____
_____
_____

Sylviette D. McGill, B.S., M.Ed., TESL

Day 32

Let's say the world is your playground, and you have every inch of it to explore and discover everything you need to know about you; how much of it have you utilized?

Date: _____

_____

_____
_____
_____
_____
_____
_____
_____
_____
_____
_____
_____
_____
_____
_____
_____
_____
_____
_____
_____
_____
_____
_____

Sylviette D. McGill, B.S., M.Ed., TESL

Day 33

Have you noticed that EVERYONE has a gift or a talent?
Identify yours and talk about what it took to discover yours; and
if you haven't, what's the thing you need to do to tap into it?

Date: _____

_____

_____
_____
_____
_____
_____
_____
_____
_____
_____
_____
_____
_____
_____
_____
_____
_____
_____
_____
_____
_____
_____
_____
_____

Sylviette D. McGill, B.S., M.Ed., TESL

Day 34

The sun rises and the sun sets.

Date: _____

_____

_____

_____

_____

_____

_____

_____

_____

_____

_____

_____

_____

_____

_____

_____

_____

_____

_____

_____

_____

_____

_____

_____

_____

Day 35

Constructive criticism. Are you the giver or the
receiver? Encourage someone today.

Date: _____

_____

_____
_____
_____
_____
_____
_____
_____
_____
_____
_____
_____
_____
_____
_____
_____
_____
_____
_____
_____
_____
_____

Sylviette D. McGill, B.S., M.Ed., TESL

Day 36

Let no man pull you low enough to hate him.

—Martin Luther King Jr.

Date: _____

_____

_____
_____
_____
_____
_____
_____
_____
_____
_____
_____
_____
_____
_____
_____
_____
_____
_____
_____
_____
_____
_____
_____

Sylviette D. McGill, B.S., M.Ed., TESL

Day 37

"To thine own self be true."

—Shakespeare

Date: _____

_____

_____
_____
_____
_____
_____
_____
_____
_____
_____
_____
_____
_____
_____
_____
_____
_____
_____
_____
_____
_____
_____
_____

Sylviette D. McGill, B.S., M.Ed., TESL

Day 38

Describe excellence.

Date: _____

_____

_____

_____

_____

_____

_____

_____

_____

_____

_____

_____

_____

_____

_____

_____

_____

_____

_____

_____

_____

_____

_____

_____

_____

_____

_____

_____

_____

Sylviette D. McGill, B.S., M.Ed., TESL

Day 39

Optimal performance.

Date: _____

Sylviette D. McGill, B.S., M.Ed., TESL

Day 40

Handle things in your life that you can control, and let God handle the rest—trust me, He handles it best!

—Sylviette D. McGill

Date: _____

Day 41

As humans, we are obviously conscious of the healing of
the body; but oftentimes, we are not in touch with the
idea of the healing of the mind, soul, and spirit.
What invisible realm is the majority of your healing taking place?

Date: _____

_____

_____
_____
_____
_____
_____
_____
_____
_____
_____
_____
_____
_____
_____
_____
_____
_____
_____
_____
_____
_____

Sylviette D. McGill, B.S., M.Ed., TESL

Day 42

From Day 41, which invisible realm is the least amount
of healing and repair taking place in your life?

Date: _____

_____

_____

_____

_____

_____

_____

_____

_____

_____

_____

_____

_____

_____

_____

_____

_____

_____

_____

_____

_____

_____

Sylviette D. McGill, B.S., M.Ed., TESL

Day 43

Be wary of competitive spirits; they're not all healthy.
Talk about the difference between the two.

Date: _____

_____

_____
_____
_____
_____
_____
_____
_____
_____
_____
_____
_____
_____
_____
_____
_____
_____
_____
_____
_____
_____
_____
_____
_____

Sylviette D. McGill, B.S., M.Ed., TESL

Day 44

Talk about your biggest weakness.

Date: _____

_____

_____
_____
_____
_____
_____
_____
_____
_____
_____
_____
_____
_____
_____
_____
_____
_____
_____
_____
_____
_____
_____
_____
_____
_____

Sylviette D. McGill, B.S., M.Ed., TESL

Day 45

Talk about your strongest personality trait.

Date: _____

_____

_____
_____
_____
_____
_____
_____
_____
_____
_____
_____
_____
_____
_____
_____
_____
_____
_____
_____
_____
_____
_____
_____
_____
_____

Day 46

It has been said that listening is the weakest communication skill. On a scale of 1 to 10 (10 being the highest), where would you rate yourself? Listen to someone today. Truly listen without thinking while they're speaking.

Date: _____

_____

_____

_____

_____

_____

_____

_____

_____

_____

_____

_____

_____

_____

_____

_____

_____

_____

_____

_____

_____

_____

Sylviette D. McGill, B.S., M.Ed., TESL

Day 47

Do you waste?

Date: _____

_____
_____
_____
_____
_____
_____
_____
_____
_____
_____
_____
_____
_____
_____
_____
_____
_____
_____
_____
_____
_____
_____
_____

Sylviette D. McGill, B.S., M.Ed., TESL

Day 48

Are you a finisher, or do you oftentimes start projects only to leave them neglected or incomplete? Do you see a reflection of this condition in your life?

Date: _____

Sylviette D. McGill, B.S., M.Ed., TESL

Day 49

Love is a universal word that people of all races, ages, and cultures use or act upon consistently. In you world/mind, what does *love* mean, and what part does it play in getting you to your better self?

Date: _____

_____

_____
_____
_____
_____
_____
_____
_____
_____
_____
_____
_____
_____
_____
_____
_____
_____
_____
_____
_____
_____

Day 50

How important is it for you to become your best self? Talk about
whether or not you feel a sense of urgency (or not) to arrive at
your better self, and why; if not, write about that instead.

Date: _____

_____

_____

_____

_____

_____

_____

_____

_____

_____

_____

_____

_____

_____

_____

_____

_____

_____

_____

_____

_____

_____

_____

Sylviette D. McGill, B.S., M.Ed., TESL

Day 51

Silence is a communication skill, just as much as talking is in my world. It's easier for some than it is others. If you are the silent type, please find yourself talking more today. Take opportunities that you otherwise wouldn't. If you are the talking type, please find yourself quiet today. Hush in situations that you would normally have the tendency to engage in. Now, write about the experience.

Date: _____

_____

_____
_____
_____
_____
_____
_____
_____
_____
_____
_____
_____
_____
_____
_____
_____
_____
_____
_____
_____
_____

Day 52

What's new in your life that you wish you
could change back to the old?

Date: _____

_____

_____
_____
_____
_____
_____
_____
_____
_____
_____
_____
_____
_____
_____
_____
_____
_____
_____
_____
_____
_____
_____
_____

Day 53

Are you a friend to yourself? If so, what type of friend?

Date: _____

_____

_____
_____
_____
_____
_____
_____
_____
_____
_____
_____
_____
_____
_____
_____
_____
_____
_____
_____
_____
_____
_____
_____
_____

Day 54

Of all the emotions that you experience in the span of a week, would you say they are even keel or overwhelming for the most part? Let's talk emotional management here. Would you say you allow your emotions or your logic to navigate you through the portals of life?

Date: _____

_____

_____
_____
_____
_____
_____
_____
_____
_____
_____
_____
_____
_____
_____
_____
_____
_____
_____
_____
_____
_____
_____

Sylviette D. McGill, B.S., M.Ed., TESL

Day 55

From Day 54, talk about the thing in your life right now that you can't seem to get a grip of emotionally. Now, let's get a game plan to get back in control of the situation and back in the driver's seat.

Date: _____

_____

_____

_____

_____

_____

_____

_____

_____

_____

_____

_____

_____

_____

_____

_____

_____

_____

_____

_____

_____

_____

_____

_____

Day 56

Giving. Write about it from a place that you are in.

Date: _____

_____

_____

_____

_____

_____

_____

_____

_____

_____

_____

_____

_____

_____

_____

_____

_____

_____

_____

_____

_____

_____

_____

_____

_____

_____

Sylviette D. McGill, B.S., M.Ed., TESL

Day 57

Selfish or selfless?

Date: _____

_____
_____
_____
_____
_____
_____
_____
_____
_____
_____
_____
_____
_____
_____
_____
_____
_____
_____
_____
_____
_____
_____
_____
_____
_____
_____

Sylviette D. McGill, B.S., M.Ed., TESL

Day 58

What is your definition of success?

Date: _____

_____

_____

_____

_____

_____

_____

_____

_____

_____

_____

_____

_____

_____

_____

_____

_____

_____

_____

_____

_____

_____

_____

_____

_____

_____

Sylviette D. McGill, B.S., M.Ed., TESL

Day 59

Are you a stranger to yourself but then seek for
someone to love a person you don't know?

Date: _____

_____

_____
_____
_____
_____
_____
_____
_____
_____
_____
_____
_____
_____
_____
_____
_____
_____
_____
_____
_____
_____
_____

Sylviette D. McGill, B.S., M.Ed., TESL

Day 60

Can you feel the better you? You are now two months
into this evolving process. Talk about your new awareness
of yourself and the things that you have shifted in
order to get to the person that you want to be.

Date: _____

_____

_____
_____
_____
_____
_____
_____
_____
_____
_____
_____
_____
_____
_____
_____
_____
_____
_____
_____
_____
_____
_____

Day 61

Born—existing as a result of birth.
Reborn—brought back to life.

Date: _____

_____

_____
_____
_____
_____
_____
_____
_____
_____
_____
_____
_____
_____
_____
_____
_____
_____
_____
_____
_____
_____
_____
_____
_____

Sylviette D. McGill, B.S., M.Ed., TESL

Day 62

It's amazing when you discover that your personal self consists of contrasting elements. For example, you can be fearless in certain areas of your life but have crippling fear on site in other areas in your life. Talk about the opposites that you deal with in your life and the plan you are implementing to rid the areas that don't move you forward to your better self.

Date: _____

_____

_____
_____
_____
_____
_____
_____
_____
_____
_____
_____
_____
_____
_____
_____
_____
_____
_____
_____

Day 63

Is there anyone you love more than yourself? And let's be clear here, we're only speaking of a healthy love, not an egotistical, selfish, better-than-anybody-else love for yourself but a genuine, authentic love. Now, what is the best way to empower yourself by increasing the love you have for you? Exactly! Did you think I was going to say lessen the love for those that you love more than yourself? Absolutely NOT! This lesson is a difficult one because now you must dig and discover what it is that's blocking you from loving yourself more.

Date: _____

_____

_____
_____
_____
_____
_____
_____
_____
_____
_____
_____
_____
_____
_____
_____
_____
_____

Sylviette D. McGill, B.S., M.Ed., TESL

Day 64

Judge not, that ye be not judged. For with what judgment ye judge, ye shall be judged: and with what measure ye mete, it shall be measured to you again. And why beholdest thou the mote that is in thy brother's eye, but considerest not the beam that is in thine own eye.

—Matt. 7 (Bible, King James Version)

Date: _____

_____

_____
_____
_____
_____
_____
_____
_____
_____
_____
_____
_____
_____
_____
_____
_____
_____
_____
_____

Day 65

This is the day that you take out the trash in your life! On separate paper, write down any hurt that you are holding on to! We are about to get the pain out of your body and its effects! After you finish writing, crying, steaming, take all that paper and burn it! Be safe, of course; I usually use my fireplace, or you can do it over a candle.

Date: _____

_____

_____
_____
_____
_____
_____
_____
_____
_____
_____
_____
_____
_____
_____
_____
_____
_____
_____
_____
_____

Day 66

Take an instance: When someone says something to you that disturbed you in the worst way, do you remember your initial reaction? Today, write about what it was that aggravated you so, and see if you can take it all the way down to the common denominator of "you!" For example, what could you have done to prevent the situation? Were you negligent in the job? It's true. Maybe the person was wrong in their handling, but it's not them we're talking about today. We're getting you to your better self.

Date: _____

_____

_____
_____
_____
_____
_____
_____
_____
_____
_____
_____
_____
_____
_____
_____
_____
_____
_____
_____

Day 67

Overwhelming! Write about it!

Date: _____

_____

_____
_____
_____
_____
_____
_____
_____
_____
_____
_____
_____
_____
_____
_____
_____
_____
_____
_____
_____
_____
_____
_____
_____

Day 68

Talk about what you are looking forward to about your better self.

Date: _____

_____

_____

_____

_____

_____

_____

_____

_____

_____

_____

_____

_____

_____

_____

_____

_____

_____

_____

_____

_____

_____

_____

_____

_____

_____

_____

_____

Sylviette D. McGill, B.S., M.Ed., TESL

Day 69

Have you accepted everything that God has in store
for you up to this very moment? If you haven't,
then what have you not accepted, and why?

Date: _____

_____

_____
_____
_____
_____
_____
_____
_____
_____
_____
_____
_____
_____
_____
_____
_____
_____
_____
_____
_____
_____
_____
_____

Day 70

As it relates to mental processing, would you say
that you have a healthy frame of mind?

Date: _____

_____

_____
_____
_____
_____
_____
_____
_____
_____
_____
_____
_____
_____
_____
_____
_____
_____
_____
_____
_____
_____
_____
_____
_____
_____

Day 71

Do you accept who you are just as readily as you
expect others to accept you? If not, why?

Date: _____

_____

_____
_____
_____
_____
_____
_____
_____
_____
_____
_____
_____
_____
_____
_____
_____
_____
_____
_____
_____
_____
_____
_____
_____

Sylviette D. McGill, B.S., M.Ed., TESL

Day 72

Health, disease, life, death, physical pain, limitations—
considering all, do you feel that your better self is achievable?

Date: _____

_____

_____
_____
_____
_____
_____
_____
_____
_____
_____
_____
_____
_____
_____
_____
_____
_____
_____
_____
_____
_____
_____

Day 73

If there is no struggle, there is no progress. Those who profess to favor freedom, and yet depreciate agitation, are men who want crops without plowing up the ground. They want rain without thunder and lightning. They want the ocean without the awful roar of its many waters. This struggle may be a moral one, or it may be a physical one, and it may be both moral and physical, but it must be a struggle. Power concedes nothing without demand. It never did and never will. Men may not get all they pay for in this world, but they must certainly pay for all they get.

—Frederick Douglass, *Narrative of the Life of Frederick Douglass*

Date: _____

_____
_____
_____
_____
_____
_____
_____
_____
_____
_____

Sylviette D. McGill, B.S., M.Ed., TESL

Day 74

Protection.

Date: _____

_____

_____
_____
_____
_____
_____
_____
_____
_____
_____
_____
_____
_____
_____
_____
_____
_____
_____
_____
_____
_____
_____
_____
_____
_____
_____

Sylviette D. McGill, B.S., M.Ed., TESL

Day 75

How do you relax? Does it come with a high price tag?

Date: _____

_____

_____

_____

_____

_____

_____

_____

_____

_____

_____

_____

_____

_____

_____

_____

_____

_____

_____

_____

_____

_____

_____

_____

Day 76

The ultimate measure of a man is not where he stands in moments of comfort and convenience, but where he stands at times of challenge and controversy.

—Martin Luther King Jr.

What is your measure?

Date: _____

_____

_____
_____
_____
_____
_____
_____
_____
_____
_____
_____
_____
_____
_____
_____
_____
_____
_____
_____

Day 77

Reflections.

Date: _____

_____

_____

_____

_____

_____

_____

_____

_____

_____

_____

_____

_____

_____

_____

_____

_____

_____

_____

_____

_____

_____

_____

_____

_____

_____

_____

Sylviette D. McGill, B.S., M.Ed., TESL

Day 78

Forgiving yourself includes what?

Date: _____

_____

_____
_____
_____
_____
_____
_____
_____
_____
_____
_____
_____
_____
_____
_____
_____
_____
_____
_____
_____
_____
_____
_____
_____

Day 79

Ladders in life.

Date: _____

_____

_____
_____
_____
_____
_____
_____
_____
_____
_____
_____
_____
_____
_____
_____
_____
_____
_____
_____
_____
_____
_____
_____
_____

Day 80

What has been your hardest lesson in life?

Date: _____

_____

_____

_____

_____

_____

_____

_____

_____

_____

_____

_____

_____

_____

_____

_____

_____

_____

_____

_____

_____

_____

_____

_____

Sylviette D. McGill, B.S., M.Ed., TESL

Day 81

Ten more days to your better self! Even though you and your life is already better because now you have taken out a lot of your emotional trash, you should definitely feel more liberated, and I am certain you feel more peace because of clutter that has been removed from inside yourself. And this is the place in the book that I should explain why I didn't title it "90 Days to Your Best Self!" We are constantly evolving, and growth is a part of our lifelong journey. Literally, you can start this same book over after ninety days, and look at the difference between the answers in your first and the answers in your second. We will be in pursuit of our best self until our time on earth is done.

Date: _____

_____

_____

_____

_____

_____

_____

_____

_____

_____

_____

_____

_____

_____

Day 82

Music.
Talk about the type of music you like, and talk about
why you think you may be attracted to it.

Date: _____

_____

_____
_____
_____
_____
_____
_____
_____
_____
_____
_____
_____
_____
_____
_____
_____
_____
_____
_____
_____
_____
_____

Day 83

"Ninety-nine percent of the failures come from people who have the habit of making excuses."

—George Washington Carver

Date: _____

_____

_____
_____
_____
_____
_____
_____
_____
_____
_____
_____
_____
_____
_____
_____
_____
_____
_____
_____
_____
_____
_____

Day 84

Have you ever committed to someone else more than you committed to yourself? You will discover the value in maintaining integrity with yourself is life-sustaining. And remember, never cheat on yourself, and always hold yourself accountable.

Date: _____

_____

_____
_____
_____
_____
_____
_____
_____
_____
_____
_____
_____
_____
_____
_____
_____
_____
_____
_____
_____
_____
_____
_____

Day 85

NOW.
Are you living a life wherein you are very present?

Date: _____

_____

_____
_____
_____
_____
_____
_____
_____
_____
_____
_____
_____
_____
_____
_____
_____
_____
_____
_____
_____
_____
_____

Day 86

"How can you get ahead if you are constantly running behind?"

—Sylviette D. McGill

Date: _____

_____

_____
_____
_____
_____
_____
_____
_____
_____
_____
_____
_____
_____
_____
_____
_____
_____
_____
_____
_____
_____

Sylviette D. McGill, B.S., M.Ed., TESL

Day 87

Are you trapped in the jail cell of your mind?
Consider beliefs that you have that limit you in your
endeavors, and talk about breaking the chains.

Date: _____

_____

_____
_____
_____
_____
_____
_____
_____
_____
_____
_____
_____
_____
_____
_____
_____
_____
_____
_____
_____
_____
_____
_____

Day 88

Facts and figures! Emotions can be mathematical.
How's the math adding up in your life?

Date: _____

_____

_____
_____
_____
_____
_____
_____
_____
_____
_____
_____
_____
_____
_____
_____
_____
_____
_____
_____
_____
_____
_____
_____
_____

Sylviette D. McGill, B.S., M.Ed., TESL

Day 89

Say hello to your better self! Talk about the top three
things that were defining during this transformation.

/ Date: _____

_____

_____
_____
_____
_____
_____
_____
_____
_____
_____
_____
_____
_____
_____
_____
_____
_____
_____
_____
_____
_____
_____
_____
_____
_____

Sylviette D. McGill, B.S., M.Ed., TESL

Day 90

Talk about what and how you plan to celebrate now that you've completed this work of self-exploration and maturation.

Date: _____

_____

_____

_____

_____

_____

_____

_____

_____

_____

_____

_____

_____

_____

_____

_____

_____

_____

_____

_____

_____

_____

_____

_____

_____

Date: _____

Date: _____

_____
_____
_____
_____
_____
_____
_____
_____
_____
_____
_____
_____
_____
_____
_____
_____
_____
_____
_____
_____
_____
_____
_____
_____
_____
_____
_____
_____
_____
_____
_____
_____
_____
_____

Sylviette D. McGill, B.S., M.Ed., TESL

Date: _____

_____

_____

_____

_____

_____

_____

_____

_____

_____

_____

_____

_____

_____

_____

_____

_____

_____

_____

_____

_____

_____

_____

_____

_____

_____

_____

_____

_____

_____

_____

Date: _____

_____

_____

_____

_____

_____

_____

_____

_____

_____

_____

_____

_____

_____

_____

_____

_____

_____

_____

_____

_____

_____

_____

_____

_____

_____

_____

_____

_____

_____

_____

Sylviette D. McGill, B.S., M.Ed., TESL

Date: _____

_____

_____

_____

_____

_____

_____

_____

_____

_____

_____

_____

_____

_____

_____

_____

_____

_____

_____

_____

_____

_____

_____

_____

_____

_____

_____

_____

_____

_____

_____

_____

_____

_____

Sylviette D. McGill, B.S., M.Ed., TESL

About the Author

Sylviette Delphine McGill—B.S., M.Ed., TEFL/TESOL—is an American editor, writer, teacher, and author who resides in Atlanta, Georgia, with her husband, Michael, as well as their two adult children and six adorable grandchildren. She loves world travel, and her passionate hobbies include gardening, photography, reading, and entertaining to name a few. Traveling the United States and abroad is one of her favorite of passions because of the wealth of learning, and experiencing a variety of cultures. After about twenty years in publishing, McGill decided to change careers and went on to pursue her M.Ed., teaching and learning. She has a love for both. She worked with individuals for more than seven years assisting them in breaking barriers in learning, processing, and applying. Teaching herself how to learn as a young child has been instrumental in her success. Sharing an array of experiences has complimented her success in teaching high school students and earned her a Teacher of the Month Award. McGill has been involved in community support and served in various capacities to help her community thrive. She has nearly two decades of publishing experience and has been awarded trophies for Soft Feature Reporting in Print and Editing in Print. McGill was also honored in *Who's Who of American Women*, Marquis Who's Who Publication, 2000–2001 Edition.

CPSIA information can be obtained
at www.ICGtesting.com
Printed in the USA
LVHW032253181220
674517LV00004B/371